This book belongs to

Presented by

Date

JB—To my children: Ashley, Andrew, Natalie, Matthew, Timothy, Bethany

NP—For Alison, Rachel, Emily, Anna, Joseph, Ben, and Jacob. I love you guys.

Text © 2014 John Bytheway
Illustrations © 2014 Nathan Pinnock
Art direction by Richard Erickson
Design by Shauna Gibby

A portion of the poem "Strange Devotion," by Walter M. Horne (in *A Pocketful of LDS Verse* [Salt Lake City: Bookcraft, 1967], 36–38) is adapted and used by permission of Deseret Book Company.

All rights reserved. No part of this book may be reproduced in any form or by any means without permission in writing from the publisher, Deseret Book Company, at permissions@deseretbook.com or P. O. Box 30178, Salt Lake City, Utah 84130. This work is not an official publication of The Church of Jesus Christ of Latter-day Saints. The views expressed herein are the responsibility of the author and do not necessarily represent the position of the Church or of Deseret Book Company.

Deseret Book is a registered trademark of Deseret Book Company.

Visit us at DeseretBook.com

Library of Congress Cataloging-in-Publication Data
ISBN 978-1-60907-790-7
(CIP data on file)

Printed in China
R. R. Donnelley, Shenzhen, Guangdong, China

10 9 8 7 6 5 4 3 2 1

THE SACRAMENT

JOHN BYTHEWAY

ILLUSTRATED BY NATHAN PINNOCK

*Inspired by the poem "Strange Devotion"
by Walter M. Horne*

Salt Lake City, Utah

When I was just a little boy, my family took a drive,

Past the buildings and the traffic, far away from city life.

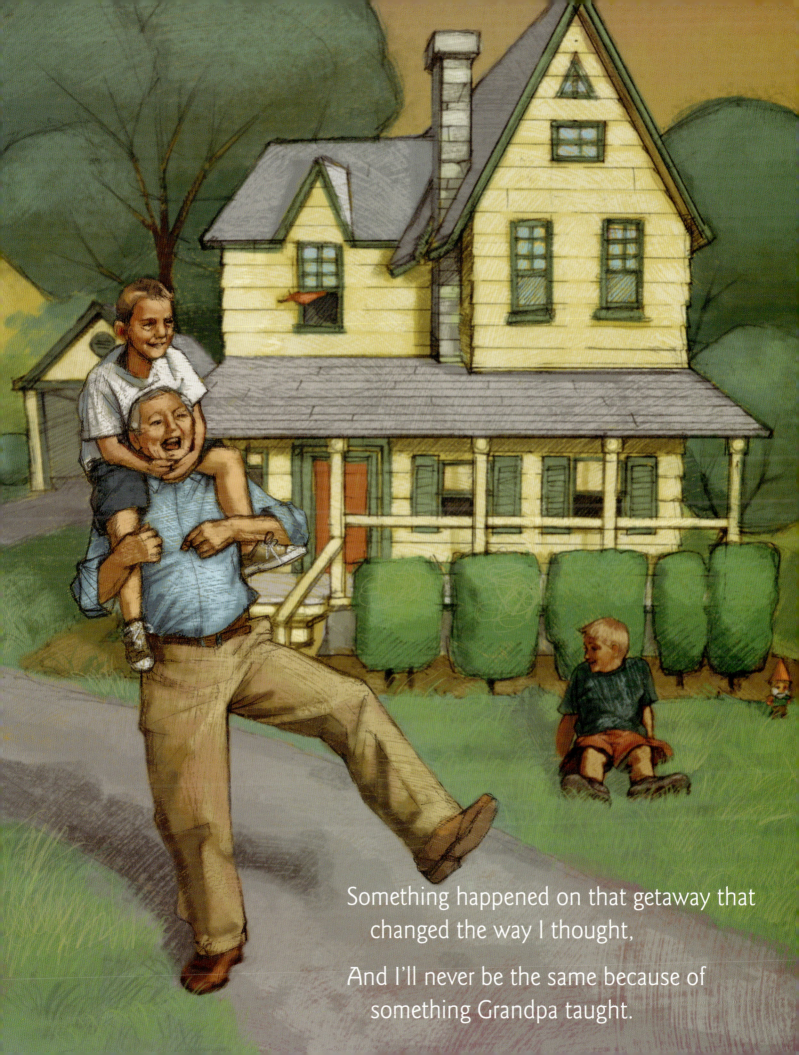

Something happened on that getaway that changed the way I thought,

And I'll never be the same because of something Grandpa taught.

As a boy on Grandpa's homestead I was happy as could be,
'Cause we'd have a picnic dinner and we'd climb the apple tree.

We'd go fishing in the river; we'd skip rocks across the stream;

And we'd watch the country sunset waiting for the stars to gleam.

Soon our Saturday was gone and though our church was far away,

Mom began preparing clothes so we could keep the Sabbath day.

'Cause "a Sunday's still a Sunday, even though we're on vacation,"

And we had to go to Grandpa's ward—amidst our celebration.

So at church I sat by Grandpa, at a loss for what to do.

Growing tired of the meeting as I slouched within my pew.

Even Mom and Dad were dozing, sometimes startled by the sound

Of little babies fussing in the chapel all around.

I had counted all the organ pipes—and all
  the choir seats—

All my pockets held were wrappers from the
  after-lesson treats.

I was flipping through the hymnbook just as
  bored as bored could be,

When my Grandpa saw me yawning and he
  softly said to me:

It wasn't very long ago, when just
   a lad like you,

I was noticing the actions of the folks
   beyond my pew—

There was envy in the glances that a lovely
   woman cast

At the hairdo of her neighbor while the
   sacrament was passed.

And a teenage girl I noticed, though a timid
   lass and shy,

Watched a youthful priest intently through
   the corner of her eye

As he sat behind the table where the water
   trays were spread—

She was not remembering Jesus nor the
   prayer the priest had said.

There was nothing reverential in the things the Cub Scout drew

On the pages of the hymnbook 'til the sacrament was through,

Not a thought of Jesus' passion entered careless elders' minds,

As they whispered to each other and the girls that sat behind,

And the high priest's brow was furrowed as he stole a secret glance

At the checkbook's dismal story of his failures in finance.

There were hundreds in the chapel but the
  worshippers were few,

And I couldn't help but wonder what the
  Lord Himself would do—

Yes, I couldn't help but wonder what the Lord
  Himself would say

Should He walk into the chapel while His
  Saints behaved this way;

Would His loving eyes be saddened; would
  His countenance be grim

While He there observed and listened to a
  service meant for Him?

When my Grandpa finished whispering,
 I knew that he was right,

And I saw a tear within his eye that sparkled
 in the light.

Suddenly I felt a glow within, a warming
 deep inside,

And the Holy Ghost was helping me
 remember Jesus died.

So that I could be forgiven of the things that I'd done wrong,

And that I could be a better boy, more humble, pure, and strong.

I'd remember there is lots of time for me to laugh and play,

But another time to worship God, to listen, and to pray.

On the morning I was baptized, I was taught that I'd be clean,
And each time I took the sacrament, I'd feel that peace again;

That repentance is a daily thing, a blessing God has given,
And our covenants are Jesus' way of bringing us to heaven.

When I see the priests and deacons and the bread and water trays,

I'll remember all my Grandpa taught me on that Sabbath day—

I'll remember Jesus loves us; I'll remember that He died;

I'll remember when I follow Him, the peace I feel inside.

I'll remember all the children that He gathered and He blessed;

I'll remember when I come to church to bring my Sunday best.

I'll remember that He lives again, and loves us still today;

I'll remember that He promised us He'll never go away.

I am thankful that I have the chance to covenant again—

That for all the Lord has done for me, I will remember Him.

Symbols of the Sacrament

The table. The sacrament table is like the table at which Jesus gave his disciples the Last Supper. Just like those disciples, we sit down in fellowship and eat with the Lord.

The sacrament table is also like an altar. An altar is where sacrifices occur, and when we use the sacrament table we remember the sacrifice Jesus made for us. In fact, one of the altars in the ancient temple was called the "table of the Lord" (Malachi 1:12; Ezekiel 41:22).

Look at the chapel in your ward building. Notice that the sacrament table is not in the back or along the side. It is in front of the chapel where everyone can see it and be reminded of its symbolism.

The cloth. A white cloth covers the bread and water trays just like the white cloth that covered Jesus' body when he was buried in the tomb. The next time you're at church, look closely at the sacrament table and see if it doesn't resemble a body covered by a cloth. Also, read John 20:7 and notice what the resurrected Jesus did with the cloth before he left the tomb.

The hymn. A hymn is like a prayer (D&C 25:12). Like the disciples, who sang a hymn at the Last Supper (Matthew 26:30), we also sing a sacrament hymn. This hymn is always about the Atonement of Jesus Christ.

The bread. The bread is a symbol of Jesus' body. The teachers don't break the bread in the sacrament preparation room, and we don't buy bread that is already in small pieces. During the sacrament hymn, the priests stand up at the table, pick up the bread, and then tear it into small pieces.

Jesus called himself the "bread of life." The priests tear the bread in pieces in remembrance of his body, which was "bruised, broken, torn for us" (*Hymns,* 1985, no. 181). The priests serve as a visual aid while the rest of us sing a hymn about the Atonement.

In the Old Testament, we read about a bread-like substance called manna that came from above and fed the children of Israel. Manna preserved their mortal lives during their wanderings. Today the sacrament reminds us that Jesus, the "bread of life," also came from above and gives us the promise of eternal life.

It's interesting to remember that the word *Bethlehem,* the place where Jesus was born, means "house of bread" (Bible Dictionary, 621).

The water. The water represents the blood of Jesus, which was shed for us. In 1830, the Lord revealed that it wasn't necessary that wine be used for the sacrament, as it was in New Testament times (see Matthew 26:27–28; D&C 27:2). Water is used today, which is also a symbol Jesus used in his teachings to describe himself and the gospel (John 4:10).

Alma may have been referring to the sacrament when he spoke of partaking of "the bread and the waters of life" (Alma 5:34). Because of Jesus' body, represented by the bread, we will all live again in the Resurrection. Because of Jesus' blood, represented by the water, we have the opportunity of eternal life.

We may be reminded of the bread and water of the sacrament when we remember that the Lord said, "This is my work and my glory—to bring to pass the immortality [which reminds us of Jesus' body, or the bread] and eternal life [which reminds us of Jesus' blood, or the water] of man" (see Moses 1:39).

Kneeling to pray. When we kneel down, it's impossible to run away. Kneeling is a posture of humility and a symbol of submitting our will to God's will. The scriptures often speak of the proud being "lifted up in the pride of [their] hearts" and wearing "stiff necks and high heads" (Jacob 2:13; 2 Nephi 26:20; Alma 4:6; Mormon 8:28). Bowing our heads is also a posture of humility and submission to God's will.

Right hand. If you had to testify in a trial, you would be required to raise your right hand and swear to tell the truth. Our right hand is our covenant-making hand. That's why, when possible, we use our right hand to take the sacrament. The sacrament helps us renew our baptismal covenants (see Russell M. Nelson, "I Have a Question," *Ensign,* March 1983, 68).

And as they were eating, Jesus took bread, and blessed it, and brake it, and gave it to the disciples, and said, Take, eat; this is my body.

And he took the cup, and gave thanks, and gave it to them, saying, Drink ye all of it;

For this is my blood of the new testament, which is shed for many for the remission of sins.

—Matthew 26:26–28